T0083124

Chord Box

Chord Box

Poems by Elizabeth Lindsey Rogers

THE UNIVERSITY OF ARKANSAS PRESS
FAYETTEVILLE • 2013

Copyright © 2013 by The University of Arkansas Press

All rights reserved
Manufactured in the United States of America

ISBN-10: 1-55728-998-0
ISBN-13: 978-1-55728-998-8

17   16   15   14   13   5   4   3   2   1

Text design by Ellen Beeler

♾ The paper used in this publication meets the minimum requirements of the American National Standard for Permanence of Paper for Printed Library Materials Z39.48-1984.

Library of Congress Cataloging-in-Publication Data

Rogers, Elizabeth Lindsey, 1985–
[Poems. Selections]
Chord box : poems / by Elizabeth Lindsey Rogers.
    pages cm
    ISBN-13: 978-1-55728-998-8 (paperback : alk. paper)
    ISBN-10: 1-55728-998-0 (paperback : alk. paper)
    I. Title.
    PS3618.O4577C46 2013
    811'.6—dc23
                                                    2012041615

Acknowledgments

Some poems have previously appeared in the following publications, some in slightly different versions:

Kenyon Review Online: "Margin, Error," "Wanted"
Pool: "人 / 入：A Redshift," "A Road in the Sky"
Crazyhorse: "罗," "鼓浪屿 *(gǔ làng yǔ)*"
Crab Orchard Review: "I-77 North: 2009," "Five Fades (II)"
Field: "In Mid-Autumn," "Length"
Seneca Review: "Elizabeth I, Richmond"
Agni Online: "Echo," "The Luthier"
Storysouth: "A Map of Shanxi"
Chautauqua Literary Journal: "New Garden"

"New Garden" appeared on Poetry Daily in September of 2007.

I want to thank everyone at the University of Arkansas Press, especially my editor, Enid Shomer, for her good faith and good advice. Thank you also to Monica Burke, who designed the cover, and to Sophie Grimes for proofreading the Chinese.

I thank Oberlin Shansi and Cornell University for their gifts of funding, experience, and time. My MFA cohort and teachers at Cornell helped with many of these poems, and Lyrae Van Clief-Stefanon helped me first see how the poems might make a book. I'm especially grateful to Alice Fulton for her vision and advice, and for giving me courage.

I'm also grateful to Martha Collins for her teaching and generosity, and for her help, in my undergraduate days, with the first poems that would become part of this book. Thanks also to Lynn Powell, Angie Estes, and Becky Gould Gibson for their encouragement, and to J. Robert Lennon, John York, and Leah Falk for their advice and friendships. And to all my friends from Shanxi—Zhao Xin, Wang Yue, Qiao Mu, Wang Hui Fang, and many others—I am forever grateful for all the hours of help with learning Mandarin, as well as with the adjustment to living in China.

Most of all, I thank my family: Dan and Lindsey Rogers, who I am blessed to call my parents, and my sisters Jennifer Rogers and Emily Pearce. And finally, to Sarah Newman, for these past six years, and for her love.

Contents

III.

I.

String Fugue with Stretto (1973–2009)

As sung to a music teacher (b. 1964)
by her student (b. 1985)

I-77 North: 2009

The blue ridge is a breve
for vowels sung in *mountain,*
the highway's long *da capo*
like a ballad you tried

to teach me. All day
I drive, taking breaths
in viaducts, tasting slack,
dry throat, valleys split

for blackness. A bridge
arches beneath me, pure
drama, bowing. This breve's
meant to hold—over

noisome runoff below—
or, as in language, to collar
words, as in distance
shortened. If you were here

you'd say next to nothing,
and make us sing
instead: about this cedar
ridge, fit for cutting

dulcimers, bodies
the shape of mountains.

You I keep singing, so
you'll hear us wound

by one long story—
even now, you wouldn't
speak of it, or know
my figure whittled out

of yours. Hum: the hollow
below, the same mine
that tracked dark
across your granddaddy's

heart and lungs,
his breath always short
until he closed up
in hardwood. I drive here,

the place you come from.
It grips, asks me to learn it
by stench. Here is the bend
where the colliery tank

turns: a radio's knob,
loud, louder where
I hold, round the curve.

Juke: 1973

Grapes cluster like blues chords
                    along the wire fence.

Your brother cuts a dry vine
                    down, wraps it tight

for smoking. At nine, you're always
                    King: outrunning all boys

from main street to the mines,
                    rattling off psalms, and you know how

to riff on whatever noise
                    your mom can find:

harmonica, piano, church-camp's
                    guitar. On your trumpet,

bell full as Loretta's big skirt,
                    you pucker for a gold

nipple, make a sound like
                    your body, but bigger. In this valley,

dim as a nightclub, you raise your chin
                    for your brother

to light the vine. Grapes glaze
              over, reflect the lit-up end.

Not ripe. You know not to eat—
              but cool, your mouth-smoke

lifting—your fingers
              twitch. You reach.

Cough: 1974

His x-ray is a lit
arch, church window
without color

and sickness spreads
in a web there, nits
cast on the open

black. In his throat
there is sound like uncut
string on the bridge,

a scraped red body
of wood, shellac
like the syrup

bottle dry.
Your whole life
you've heard this

metal spoon
and its sudden chime
in the sink,

wind half-
caught in fold.
He sleeps. Sunday

and Wednesday
nights spent in
the armchair,

spittle jammed
into breast-pocket,
hardening to an ash.

Dirge: Autumn 1974

The bell, your granddaddy says,
must point toward the casket.
He shifts into a higher

gear, reaches for your
blue lapel, the only dark
thing you own. He lent

you his tarnished star,
spelled *American Legion,*
pinned it to your budding

chest. When he lingers
here, you flinch. His hand
glosses your newest, doubled

sting, the pucker beneath
your jacket, as if a black widow's
bitten twice. Your lungs

tighten. *I'm proud
of you* he says, edging up
to the cemetery, a ridge

unveiled suddenly
from the pulling wool
of clouds. In the grass,

for an unknown veteran
you play "Taps": one stop,
broken chord, first song learned

on trumpet. You know enough
to let the C come deferred
like anguish, to give G its high

fermata, ⌒ the bird's eye
on where you stand
among the old, blue

and black shoulders
beneath trees, leaves
turning to brass.

Belt: 1975

Part southern, part rust
    belt: in Huntington, train tracks suture

down the Ohio River's
    dingy skein. Eleven years old, on Tuesday evenings

you watch smokestacks spew
    sinister questions; you listen

to the untuned bass of tires
    as your granddaddy drives

across one bridge, then
    another. Still, some beauty left

here—on the flood bank, a row of houses
    he calls *painted ladies,* and in the blue one

your own guitar teacher files
    snags from your nails, speaks Italian

names for each finger.
    You have never spoken

like this, with richness held
    to your tongue, never had

a more refined tone on the guitar
         than now, that angle he trains

in your hand. The rasp and plink
         you taught yourself at home

lengthen to *cantabile*
         with the right blend

of flesh-to-nail.
         Tell me about your lesson

Granddaddy asks, driving you
         home, tugs your wrist

to his lap, and the gape
         below the buckle. Your mouth recites

names as they harden
         into amber. The town

passes, grays in your window,
         night coming, with metal in the teeth.

Prelude for Open Strings: 2000

An E and an E, one high and one low,
and four in between—an E sandwich.

We learned the upper strings first, fumbling
through mini-tunes, one-liners, like a run

around the block: passing F and G,
sprinting to C and D, but always an end:

E. Our first guitars were tinny, made
like the craft-of-the-month in *Highlights Magazine*

for Children, where you took scissors to a shoebox,
strung it with rubber bands. The high E

was the worst, like a whining child—
angular, temperamental. You turned to me

wanting the class in tune:
give us an E. For elementary, but

also the potential for eminence
and elegance, and for Elizabeth.

It was evident: you had visions
for me. Long after the others

had gone on to second period,
I sat still while you filed

my nails, smoothed the crests
with your buffing cloth.

After that, notes hummed
under my fingers. Easy.

p—i—m—a: 2001

pulgar, indice, medio, anular:
names of the fingers
on the right hand. *p*
is the thumb, *the big one.*

That's disgusting
I said. The boys smirked
and laughed. *a* is the ring
finger, where the nail grows

strongest, the sound as full
as the vowel itself: *ah.*
There's middle *m,* who never
plays alone, always alternating

with *i* on the left, who stands
for *has issues.* I'd file
and give it exercises—
limited results. *i* was hesitant,

indefinite—like an imaginary
number from algebra class.
Be patient you said, your best
teacher's voice. We couldn't

call you by your first name:
T—i, but knew it finished

with that unruly letter.
Your signature was *T*

with a tail, nothing else seen
except the dot of *i,* hovering above
an ink line—like some wild note
broken off the melody.

Ensemble: 2001

We named our trio the Parallel Dreamers
because Amanda was an Aquarian, born
in a mountain town, and because Kat

said the other kids called us hippies.
But mostly it was that we dreamed
in similar scenes—the nightmare of playing

a concert naked, or one where the guitar
shatters. And at least once, although
we were embarrassed to admit it

we'd all woken with a memory
of our teacher's hands. I never mentioned
that once you'd said *I dreamt of you, too,*

or how I'd opened my mouth in the contour
of a question. But by then class had begun;
you were taking the morning's attendance,

penciling new fingerings into our trio's
score. *Beth, Kat, Amanda*—you'd call us
as an entity, like spelling a chord:

tonic, mediant, dominant. We were
Scorpio, Aquarius, Taurus—a trinity.
There's water and air, you said. *You are earth.*

Hold fast to my hand. Listen.
You are never to play second
guitar—only the bass line, or melody.

Vibrato: 2001

Like this, you said,
wiggling the flesh
at the center of my
palm, but it was months

before I learned. There, at the heart
of a simple sarabande
the high A first

trembled in the hollow
of my hand. My fingers
like cathedral beams

where a voice wafted—
callow, but clear,
though the song itself

was old. *That was beautiful*
you said. *In all my years*

I've never had a student
who just knew . . .

I held that last note
until the wind began
to shudder outside

your office window. *Look,*
you said, *you made it rain, see*

beads quivering above the sill
like a descant; your hand

drifts across my throat,
shoulder, and thigh—*Why is it*

that you're trembling? I said I cannot
be still. Nothing here

will hold. I'm quaking down
beneath the bone, where

my marrow, darkly
contralto, is humming.

Psalm: 1976

You unlatch

the dark guitar case
on your bedroom's

braided rug, which looks
like the God's eye ◈

you wound in Sunday School
as you sang: *blessed*

are they whose ways are
blameless. Open my eyes

so that I may see.
Your mother hung it

in your window, where
she looms now,

then grabs your arm:
If you ever tell

sick lies again—
not calling him

Granddaddy but instead
my father. Then nothing

but her slippers
slapping, dead

stop at the corner
where hall bends

into stairs. Air catches
like a locket on her throat

the full minute she stands
by the banister, not

going. You blink,
unlock the stare

on black and white
copied pages, where

the bottom line's played
pedal point, half notes

tied like cheap pearls.
You start the song

with the door left
open, so that

she, in some other
room, can hear.

Duet in E minor: 2002

Cold weather, we agreed, was bad
for the instrument. All winter long

you'd driven me to my car, as if
dark Capricorn evenings, almost

sinister, could split a soundboard
in a single, seismic instant. The truth is

January's mild in our town; often I wore
that scarf just because you'd smooth it

with the back of your hand, then drift
up to my girl-glossed lips: *Sweetness, you*

look so good in brown. Come March,
there were fewer excuses. Every day I drove

with my windows down, the air blowing
both ways, like the high E and the low,

struck at the same moment—their ringing
enveloped me. I called you

and asked, *is it possible for you to love*
two at once, and your *yes* was like your arm

when it conducted the ensemble—a clear
source of authority. I knew Anna,

the woman you'd loved for eleven years;
she was my dance teacher. On Fridays

after my music lesson, I'd wear
her helmet, two sizes too large, riding

on the back of your Honda. That spring,
I learned wind from all sides.

Pastoral: 2002

Free and clear? I wondered, as May finished
in a furious cadenza, the rhythm of that year

coming undone. Along 220 North, the kudzu
erupted into an archipelago of notes, levitating

in bottle-colored clusters. My whole body
rang. At sixteen, seventeen, my lessons

were followed by long drives near
the county line, where I relearned all

that was linear. Through July you traced the V
between my thighs; the sun throbbed

through the windshield. Sting
on the radio.

Do you know this song? It was '85
you said, and meant college, the conservatory,

your junior recital. In your office
there was a picture in which you wore

a tuxedo and, like an emblem, a guitar.
When you're young, you said, the fall from grace

goes quickly, so you can stand up again
without losing much time. I said '85,

that's the year I was born,
and you didn't reply. But like fret

after fret, I could sense
heaviness, and a measured descent. You placed

your hand back on the wheel, and turned.

Aubade, Falsetto: 1978

Thirteen, and nearly deaf
in the left ear, very little

wakes you. Your good side
against the pillow

mutes the early timbres.
You don't hear birds

or your brother's light feet
as he leaves with Granddaddy

and your father
for the first spring hunt.

Or their rifles, the crackling
softened by distance.

Two years before
you would've begged

to go, but now prefer
sleep, its feverish meter

through the morning.
You aren't awake to know

wisteria, the scent
witching your nose

like a girl's
tendrils. You are dreaming

of Grace, your friend
with the honey hair

and her spoken
alto, somehow lifted

into descant.
In her right hand, a wafting

cigarette. The other fist
full of feathers—barred,

perhaps a hawk's.
She moves towards you,

what you've longed for—
a god where breath

meets breath. Sleep: both ardor
and refuge. When you stir

you find last night's
phone, forgotten

in the crook
of your shoulder.

Where her voice
was, a siren answers—

clamoring, reed-like
as you wake.

Chorale: 1979

It feels full,
holy—blue ridge

white with
winter,

hills lining up
in their habits

of snow.
So the last

place you want
is down here

in this lot,
ledger lines

near gone, fine

powder under ice.
Don't touch—

you will not
see her again

he says, pulling over
as if the eye

⌒

was a margin
to be held.

She, head
of the band

kept time
with boots

lifting—
bound, as in

deer, knee-high
in the drift.

You will not inherit.

You lifted, then,
her A-line, hand

over hand like rope
while the next

room's choir
was strangely

tacit, only
rustling robes.

Your mother

will see to this.
You want, now,

out——to jump

the nearly-
buried fence.

False Cadence: 2002

Under sharp
       shoulder blades, two

knots hid, twins
       behind the bone. Once, you

grazed the left
       along your thumb, had the right
under your pinkie,
       the finger we rarely used.

That was a real beginning:
       your span a two-

pronged shadow—
       a wishbone. Who yanked? We both

knew my back tightened—
       it was not the hours
pressed against
       the window, slurs and

scales—but because that first instrument
       I'd been given

was so full
       across the bout, too large for me to handle.

Your phone rang. You snared
         along its cord:

                              I talk to you more

                                        than my sister. Don't act

                    like a child. Do you know

                                        what I've risked?

                    for you?

Once, I'd taken
         your picture, tried to
capture your A-string's
         vibrato—it was easy, in that blur

to say your hand
         was like a sparrow.

That warm morning
         in autumn, I roused

my tantrum
         half. I hissed

when you opened
         the car door, windows
wiped clean of color.

                              I never said I love

you said. Your face wet salt.
       My voice raised,
my first threat:

I could tell.

You yanked
       me by the wrist.
My fingers, then,

cupped, or clenched
       between your breasts.

Leading Tone: 2002

That final autumn, you'd given me
Paganini's *Romanza,* saying, learn

this. I'd want it for auditions.
It was the hardest piece

I'd ever played, and, in time,
I knew it better

than you did. I remember
evening light, heavy

with the color
of apples—I played the piece

for all of your studio.
The coda's bass line twinged

rubato, A minor descending
to murmurs, then

nothing. That moment, I hated
you, couldn't bear how still

they were. I said, the B section's
wrong; did you hear my buzzes

among the low notes?
It's a guitar,

a student replied, what do you expect?
I couldn't answer, couldn't look

at you. What should I
have said, my mouth

as it screwed up, and my gut
playing *ponticello,* which means *near*

the bridge: the rawest sound
on stringed instruments.

To the Conservatory: 1983

Is it you now, driving down—
no, it is you being driven—south
thru Beckley, Big Walker, Wytheville,

towns ticking off like longs & breves.
Since you and your mother
have nothing, by now, to say,

it is safe to crown yourself king & queen
of Gomorrah, and to your cropped
hair, lift the snake of your headphones.

Olivia demands *let me hear*
your body talk. At eighteen, what more
could yours say? You pulse

to the thought of her strut, a saint
in a white leotard and headband.
It must be your father at the wheel. Mother,

looking lost—blinded by August, slurring
past the window. For a moment, she turns
to the back, her glance meeting yours.

She, too, has beautiful hands.
On the piano, more than an octave's
reach—and a clearer voice

than yours, a round room
with mandolin thrumming.
You will not hear her now, cowering

beneath your headphones. Both of you
looking to the other side
of glass, where it's hard, now, to tell

the difference: mountain from the berm.
Carolina arrives, the hills starting
to level—*he makes me lie*

down—is she singing?—
in green pastures. Soon,
in a new room, you'll undo

this black lung, lift the guitar
neck from that muteness
in the traveling case. When she leaves

you here, she will know enough
not to offer you
her psalters. She knows, too, the slope

of both shoulders, and how long
the salt's been spilled.

Coda: 2003

All the way up to Ohio, the guitar
was strange, posed

in the back seat
like a hitchhiker. The day before

I'd cracked my *m* nail
while I was packing, having no choice

but to file it down
to its bed, where anything that touches

stings. The drive north
was full of mountains, and all morning

the landscape rose
in perpetual modulation, a practiced

scale. Back home, I knew
you might be thinking

of me; you had risen
and were drinking coffee

at the kitchen table,
Anna singing at the skillet,

frying eggs. At dinner
the night before, you'd both given me

a necklace strung
from your favorite earrings: a dancing woman,

and a guitar, with a small stone
between them: green. Anna said, *you have no idea*

how much lies
ahead of you, but what

could she know, as you glanced
over for the last time,

suspending me—eighteen
then, perhaps still—

etched in your mind's
eye. In exchange for mastery

of his instruments, it's rumored
that Paganini made a pact

with the devil, and often
I've wondered what

I gave up, learning to
play guitar: something

lost, or something rendered
willingly. We love the cadence

not just because it resolves,
but because we're taught

that dissonance signals
an end. Crossing the river

into Ohio, I saw hills line up
like a choir, and remembered

what you told me: singers
are the luckiest. No voice is like another.

With the radio, I loose
mine, let it hover

between registers.
Your arm, a ghost—

weight first—
now, air where it lifts.

II.

Elizabeth I, Richmond

Damp nights, pearwood pegs
wouldn't keep long

without slipping; if she had
an hour to play, she'd spend

half of it just to tune. Mist
like a parchment held

the Thames, two banks drawn
as tablature. She took a lute

not for performance, but to shun
melancholy alone in her chambers.

She'd asked again
for solitude. Virginals

couldn't be moved, but
this instrument could be

carried into a vacant
room. She was tired

of the fawning over
her hand's long

reach—how her lady's
index could bar ebony

whole. *I seem stark mute,*
but inwardly do prate:

she wrote first and then
for voicing, drew a breve

on figured bass. This
was the only way a man's

timbre might enter
the room: her hand, a foil

against page, and plucking
tied gut, knots on the rose.

Echo

After Antigoni Goni performing Brouwer's "La Huída de los Amantes por el Valle de los Ecos"

To turn back at the hill, or wall—
all dogs will come home.
all sons arrive, their pockets torn.

A mirror: Narcissus drinks
blue ink from the stream
and cannot leave. I love you

I love you since to imitate
is a pattern learned, call for
yes again: a voice is made

by doubling. Lungs lift
against the chord
box, stir its twin folds.

Antigoni Goni's hands
butterfly across the fretboard,
neck where strings pull

like latitude through dark.
In her song, the lovers flee—
horses' hooves accelerate

down to the valley—and before
they are caught, they call out.

Five Fades

(I)

Bent over testicular tomatoes
and the hairy vines of squashes,
she had gone out for an hour
to escape the sick-bean smell
of the kitchen. Inside, he dozed,
the radio fuzzy, Lynchburg
his honeybee. The snores
whisked out of his sickled lips.
He was dreaming of earthquakes.
A clock tower crashed through
the barn roof, its idle hands—
sharp as Satan's—still ticking.

(II)

We wouldn't walk barefoot
over that linoleum floor,
the tawny argyle
of a copperhead's back.
We wouldn't touch
anything—not the mirror
that swung or the Precambrian
Vasoline, wouldn't ask
about the Country Crock tub
with overripe banana peels
on the back of the commode.

48

We didn't want to think of them
gray and naked in there—
her behind frosted glass
or him sunk in the tub.
I drew the curtain
so Jesus In a Jar wouldn't look
while I peed. Bent down
to the floor, I crossed my eyes,
backed away from the dangers
of this geometry, waiting
for the magic-eye, the image
to jump out.

(III)
He kept a shrine to Reagan
in the tractor shed. Do not take her

back there she'd yelled at him but still
beyond the pitchfork and cans of stain

he tugged my hand through one-hinged,
walls closing in with a pin-up's purple

fade. Was the ceiling sloped
or was his cowboy hat cocked? In the Reaganless

spots, calendar photos of the Cascades,
or animals in danger. A far blue mountain

tucked into closer black
was how plaid disappeared

into his belt line.
When he called my name

I kept my elbows
held out—and cut

quick across the corner
with the gray wolf's head thrown back.

(IV)
Between the preserves and crockery

she kept her vanity's copper key.

I took a velvet seat and fit

clover to clover. Right drawer

opened full to cotillion gloves

and winter sleeves for attaching,

the left with her scissors, snuff-tin,

and two cuspids on a sliver

of wire. I couldn't read the cursive

in blue-lined letters but guessed

something high and fake in those helium o's.

In her brown kitchen, tea made ice

chatter at jar's bottom. When I was called

to grace, I smelled like gone-sour.

Have you washed your hands? He cut

a cold biscuit to spread with peaches,

asked her his favorite question: remember

your birthday, the one when Kennedy

was shot? When she opened to say yes, I saw

what she had been missing—without the silver

retainer, or his half-dollar put in its place.

(V)
   After Andrew Wyeth

My grandfather kept his acres
with a buzzing wire
            fence, and a grove

of sweaty magnolias
drawing the most opaque
            shadows I've known. Almost frost

beneath, despite heat
that clabbered your blood.
            Even the concrete porch

felt more like a fossil
than it did good living.
            In the farmhouse, he napped

to Rush and Jerry's
drone. Faded prints
            formed a triptych:

the first an auburn Jesus,
hands folded in prayer.
             The second Jesus leaned

his head against a fishing net—
posed, it was hard to tell
             if he'd walked on water, or suddenly

cameoed as the surfer
in a Juicy Fruit commercial.
                         The third was *Christina's World*—

I confused her first
for Mary—her limbs gray and twisted
             as an orchard's in winter.

Don't stare. A few children
came to church in a special van.
                   They sang "He-e-e's alive!"

clapping off the beat.
My grandfather under his breath:
             God's punishment, then *mothers'.*

My grandma sucked in
her breath, and, turning
                   away from him, said nothing.

Later, she canned
preserves, pinched raw
             pie crusts. On her feet, bunions

bulged through nylon.
She sent me out with a bag
            to snatch the windfall pecans.

I tried to imagine a field
open as Christina's, without
            its edges hemmed

in overbearing trees.
But I knew that spiral down
            her spine. It was the way

oak leaves let go. I knew
that dead-sea distance
            between the farm and girl.

New Garden

Gentle as doves, and *wise like*
serpents, but what knowledge,
we ask, might this animal have?

The brain is just a seed,
a weight barely felt, not like
our own—a house with an attic

and cellar, where volumes
lie in their mantles of dust,
long untouched by hand or sun.

The snake does not know what it is
to remember. His heart, a simple
matter—three adjoining rooms.

What we hold in our fourth,
called *ophidiophobia,* is the fear
of sting, and what the Book said.

My father warned me of copperheads:
Walk away, he said, *and do not scream.*
And I was twenty, home in the spring,

when I saw my first,
coiled by the tiger lilies.
I was alone and gawked

at the burnished beauty—that alien
alphabet of hourglasses, drawn
in colors of blood and earth.

A snake is a thing without a left lung.
Long ago, it was surrendered
for the sake of moving forward.

And had we given ours,
would we have more room
for our apple hearts, so pent-up in rib?

A woman told me this:
to come of age is to recognize
the myths we were taught.

Margin, Error

Vincenzo Galilei (1520–1591), lutenist, composer, music theorist,
and father of Galileo Galilei

The numbers always failed
when forced with heaven's
weight: *absolute, holy*—

what about the gut, and its unknown
flaws—if an octave is perfect
then why the fifth impure?

Galilei picks up where Pythagoras
tossed his hammer to the sand,
having sketched the first crude ratios

from a water glass and a row of bells.
But what is rational in day
by night is spun back

to question—and so in the dim
of his studio, Galilei's work
is all refrain.

Again with ballast
he ties and plucks, asks God
to foil muteness. Squaring

weights: two to four,
three to nine—the intervals pronounce
just as they slip, their dissonance

slight as heartbeat.
Poised with pen,
he stutters through

the figure. This ratio
of tension and octave
not, in fact, Pythagorean

2:1, but more abstruse:
varying with square root, and also
instinct. Sonority—

a capricious code—casts,
recasts in human form.
He stirs in his chair. What note,

he thinks, is not played
tremblingly, or untunes
from bloating wood—it's summer,

the Arno hisses. A rough
watermark, this new equation,
one of nearly-, almost:

chaos. Despite the late hour,
it seems noisy in this house,
and every house. Walls echo

with the children's arguments,
scratching pens, the squeak
of their compass. So unsettled, all of them—

stirring nights with their questions,
and awake again before
dawn, already thumbing at lutes.

The Luthier

Antonio de Torres Jurado (1817–1892), Spanish guitar maker

Torres's secret was
soundboard, made
like a corset: cypress

struts that narrowed
at the waist. After
his wife was buried

in pine, he locked
all doors but
one—landing's

lead-up to roof,
where cut spruce
aged from bone

to honey. Window
was frame for sea's
dull sawing, while

his good ear kept
time in waves. At noon
he called the boy,

taught him to slit
the sanded neck,
how to hold a needle

still enough for rosette's
slow ticking. Herringbone,
he showed him, is hardest

on old hands, for
only a precise grip
of dark veneer

can lay down
this ring, sign
without sound.

A Road in the Sky

ITHACA, NY

It wouldn't be held—
this notion, slipknot

spring—park that pushed
its own banks, spilled vines

over the lookout. O North
I've never understood, capricious

cloud and gaze, lush
and then snow, that snap-

dragon give & take. But we were warm

a moment, and still on
our backs, where winter grass questioned

the margins of skin, and trees tossed
dark like paper cutouts, or lace that ripped

if spoken of too soon.
I am the screen, she said, *on which*

you throw your passion,
as if I'd rendered her

a level plane
to call an interruption. If that, then

what was my language? *Please, please:*

raw color without
conduit, the buttercups'

fevered form. Perhaps it's true

that what had drawn me
to her, at first, was reflection: narcissus

eye on eye, dart pressed
to dart. Collar turned back

when she allowed me
to open it, let my hand

be the bearing
towards—visible, or not—whatever cyan

we might cross. In that pivot

from day to black, a blinking jet
traced an axis above us, and I said

to her, the pilot's
daughter: *cut the veil;* even the sky

feels owned. How easily

she lifted the aqua hem
of my dress, but scolded

when I moved
closer, etched my face

into her skin. This was the map: my willing

mouth parted, tasting wild
yonder, her hair's bitter oat.

Nodes

David Rubio (1934–2000), British maker of stringed instruments

In 1787, Ernst Chladni discovered consistent visual patterns by strewing sand on vibrating plates and watching it collect along nodal lines.

—*Springer Handbook of Acoustics*

At a café in Seville, troubadours
read his grounds:
go home; use tools; your red beard

will grow long.
For thirty years, he bent Tilia
to irons, met the edges

with hide glue.
Nest, his wife,
in her nook whirred

looms: rugs were color—
or warmth—for corners
not consumed

in wood curl.
He chiseled to her sounds.
He moved as she moved.

To test a soundboard's
resonance, he'd open the tin
of tea—and scatter leaves

like ash, revving the synth
to the desired pitch.
On G_3, leaves stirred—slowly,

as if post-mortem—and with
the precision of woodwork,
they drew a navel, encircled: ☉

In a cup, or natal chart
it should be read
as a sun. Light, will, love

a life's work—and in time
one's own undoing. A tumor he
could touch, roundness in his neck.

There was a glyph in the mug
the day he died. It was ♓,
the way leaves trace

G_2—two fish back
to back, cambered
but looped together.

She felt this without
knowing: the minute
he sunk to his table. October,

trees lowering their flame
and blond. She rose
from her loom, found his face

in sawdust—an inch
from the last instrument,
left without its varnish.

Here, her arc begins.
She is still, but grief bends
towards her. The scissors

clasped in one
hand, red thread
wound in her other.

Floater (Myodesopsia)

*On the subject of 3-D universes floating in 4-D space . . . to what
extent your astral body is connected to your physical body is
unclear in the writings I have consulted.*
—*Rudolf v.B. Rucker,*
Geometry, Relativity, and the Fourth Dimension

Shadow of a hair. Seen in blank's
monochrome: wall or sky. What curls
up like absence, or a cobweb yanked

by a head crown. Spiral
after the blink: *Muscae volitantes:*
fly's flying. Not the body, but the whorl

in its leaving. One of us says
I see out of the corner while the other
doesn't see. Between retina and lens, say

gel suspends belief. Our mother
cannot be ghost. We must be very tired.
Collagen as a line finds no other

explanation. But the quagmire
is vitreous matter, fixed
but not at rest. It takes a while to find a wire

with the hyperbola inside. The trick
is on the eye, a scrim
lit front and behind. Tick

is not our dimension. A rim:
what little we see. Space
turns, a still in the moving dim.

III.

A Map of Shanxi

SHANXI PROVINCE, CHINA, 2007

First, draw the world.

But the world
erased of water. Lake bottom,

now a plateau. Riverbed, arc

of dust. And where ocean should be,
a swaying tapestry of corn.

To make TH, I tell my students,
the tongue must curl
and leave the mouth. *Think this*

through: northern earth's

weather. Repeat until tongues
harden, parch like the valley

of Ezekiel. Voices elbow
towards a cadence. Words
hit words, pile like skeletons.

And all day, the air's *gānzào*—
so dry, I can't feel what it is

you might call God. As if to say

it's humid were a synonym

for knowing the hand,
the sweaty familiar hold of it, lines

that are rivers. No, my skin splits

in absence. We ride
on, bikes veiled

in thirsty powder. Gobi wind
takes the leaves, leaves us still,

and wanting—what

was it? A forgotten word

tastes like
the barrel's bottom.

Frantic to remember,
all I know is to head towards
the market, in hopes

someone might have it
in their cracking hand,
so I can ask, *what is this?*

But here, without
the word, I've forgotten
also the shape of it,

and what else is there
to recall now, in this place

where every color is living

the life of another? I buy oranges
but they're green. Greens

are prisms, spun in oil. Egg yolk,
something blue. My hair, dull

auburn, students calling
gold. I told the vendor

I need   I *was* needing

or was it?   Was it
wanting,

either, the same character:

yào. 要 Open your mouth,
let the wind out

and then on closing, find it

empty. The dry mouth
that first asked *where*

is the cup, my crude
mouth that also said

the sky looks backwashed
in watercolor

is now searching for
the bright word, waiting

in the dust. If Ezekiel

wants the wheel, it's the cigarette-
sun, setting on Shanxi,

neon on inhale, black by the time
the lips separate again. *Think this*

through: northern earth,

speak. An echo is just
a voice, just the bones,

your own. Write a name
in loess, watch it leave

you, slip behind the atlas.

Cup your hands, and wait.
But do not ask for rain.

罗

BEIJING, 2007

热 meant *hot,* summer's
tin sky, city grid
closed in, a mesh:

hemmed. Only that
one street had green
relief of trees, and a few

popsicle chests: flavored
mung bean, hawthorn,
corn. Even jokes on a stick

I couldn't write or read.
Why are the neighbors'
parrots hung in cages

along the road? I would
have asked Teacher Hé
had I had the right

verbs. Instead I cupped
one hand in the shape
of a hemp room, and

with the other pointed:
bird, them, why.
Because they too need air

she said, *whoosh*
to make meaning clear;
to catch a breeze

men played blackjack
with their shirts half-
lifted. Parrots rocked,

almost reticent
except the occasional
易易: *yì yì* from the trees.

Almost *yī*, which
means *one*. At first
I resisted the pen

as her hand gripped
mine, covered its rock
like paper. We etched

my new surname,
spun its fine
black thread:

罗:　　　*luó*

a lifted net, a gauze
for catching birds.

In Mid-Autumn
SHANXI PROVINCE, 2007

After Du Fu, for Sarah

The moon was not

        the moon

but it was, it was moon

        yes, and cake,

            yuè bǐng.

bing, I cried.   *ice*   or *sickness*

        depending, *sweet*

heart, you are still where   you are. the kitchen

      again, the cricket's

        vibrato in the sink.

the onion turned,

      blushed

        by the window.

Sick, a hush,

      slides on bathroom

tile, blue

        and white,

            ice   alone

finds its way   to bed.

yuè, I said.   *moon*

            or breathing

                you. Come,

    draw the circle. Reach

              north, where I stand.

Night   is the syrup,

              cupped between our hands.

人 / λ : A Redshift

Rén: (人): (Mandarin) man, person, people, someone else

*Lambda (λ): Eleventh letter of the Greek alphabet, used in
mathematical functions, and to represent wavelengths, growth
rates, and unity, among other meanings.*

A single person, the body's
pictograph. A human standing up 人

after hours of lying down.
All night on the train

we slept a slow arrow 人
through darkness, and in morning

Chinese discovered me: carrot- 人
headed, unaccompanied.

你一个人吗?

Are you a person? I 人
was asked, but meaning

one: are you alone.
I was. It'd been a half-year

since I had another person 亻

(lying down) and yet
I'd been brushed

by thousands:
crowned with dynamite's

wick, standing in   𝛌
for many, the People's Republic

of Population. Not an inch
in any room, but out the window

we saw thirty-six hours   𝛌
of next-to-

nothing—the Mongolian border
grass shifting, wavering   𝛌

in its graph. It's math, an empty set:

a lone tree, one hand cracked.
Not only were you not here

I knew you would never
want to be—in this slow Doppler   𝛌

of old men, who pointed out

what I (on my own)
might have missed: *here's the red-flecked*

bushes, these 麻 *peppercorns*
that numb, the mild electric 人

current you can touch
against your tongue.

The more we spoke
the more people that gathered

and like some failed
constant, our din 人

grew as we traveled, as the whistle
cried and changed pitch

through a town, came close 人

and then behind us—
人 , or daylight pulled away.

At the Bathhouse
SHANXI PROVINCE, 2008

for Qiao Mu and Wang Hui Fang

Even among friends, I can't make light
    of my body. With calculated slowness—
half-ecclesiastical, half-shy—I unzip,
    loosen buttons, undo my hook
from its eye. Fog halos the doorway, but don't
    call this a vision. Plastic-sandaled,
we edge through the crowd—all elbows
    and angles, more chaos than Euclidean.

Learn shame: bare your American ass
    to a room of Chinese women. "So big!" My friends giggle
when it nudges them without permission.
    "Your country loves beef and bread," the denim seller
once said to me. She recommends dark jeans
    to the voluptuous. "This will hide your hips."

Wang Hui Fang passes me the bottle,
    shampoo that reeks of something
freesia. The three of us trade
    back-lathers, suds from nape to waist.
Six, seven women ring
    each spigot. I don't know the best phrase
for *excuse me.* "Oh, just push people out of the way,"
    my friends say when I wait to rinse.

Black hair swirls, turns along
     its Coriolis, then mats to a mink
where the attendant sweeps it off the drain.
     To work, she's only in underpants
and a jade pendant on a string.
     "Does she feel embarrassed?" I ask.
On my forehead, Qiao Mu twirls a wet tendril.
     "Why?" she asks. "We're all women."

For the full-bodied scrub, we lie
     face-down on cellophane. I hold
my breath when the woman
     stands behind me. Never mind I would never
let a lover look at me in this position.

My breasts sweat into plastic.
     Under her mitted hand,
I flinch. Dead skin pills
     like a cheap sweater.
There's that tepid
     shock, the bucket's
final pour. "Now flip," she says,
     slaps the small of me.

Wanted

SHANXI PROVINCE, 2009

Dusk, dogs grunt
behind the closed
mud of courtyards

to tell me I shouldn't
be here, that this
is no place to be

alone. At school
the wanted poster
had a blurry inkblot

stare, reminding me
of easy characters
I still can't read

hand-written.
Get your organs harvested
was the rough relay

of meaning,
and so I run past
the brick factory,

the empty
Uighur restaurant,
and kilometers

of wheat, silence
like missing skin. On
the edge of town, parlors

are turning on
halogen signs,
按摩: *massage*

for less than the price
of dinner. I'm warned
by 按, a portrait

of a woman kneeling
down, and 摩,
to rub, a hemp house

with 手 inside: *hand.*
Night hours especially
females shouldn't

move alone:
if you are here
after dark, you're looking

or looked for. Dogs
as I hurry home,
cross the outer

wall of town. A girl
washes her face, spits
into the alley. Mother—

still in veil—keeps
an eye from the door
until the child runs

towards her, reaching
her palms to face.
摸 *: to touch, to feel,* drawn

as a hand beside this
莫: the sun as it slips,
disappears into the brush.

鼓浪屿 *(gǔ làng yǔ)*
IN FUJIAN PROVINCE, ALSO KNOWN AS "THE ISLAND OF PIANOS"

To learn the God
of an island, I listen first

for his hammers:
here, the thimble-drop

of bougainvillea, and mollusks
clicking in silver bowls.

Boats, a row of Dutch shoes,
clap, hull

against hull—along
the reef, what is heard

       as timpani: 鼓浪屿, *gǔ làng yǔ*—
鼓 *drum,* 浪 *wave,* 屿 *islet.*

Once, *eyelet:* Sunday's lace
and *swish*

when white ladies
landed, arms buried

under hymnbooks.
      They came with pianos

to dolly-up the island
hills, and to form

chorales from orphans,
mining belief

like ore. Faith, quick to cull

in a sturdy room
of sound—everyone can love

4/4, the easy symmetry
in hymns.

                    My shadow grows a train
as I wander, wrap around

porches—and snake through
alleys, where Tuscan villas

mold and yellow.
Moon-shaped gates

are the old rings
to someone's garden—and over trees

Koxinga stands on a peak
in granite armor.

喵喵: *miāo miāo*
a peacock shrieks, splays

his tutu of evil eyes.
Is this some sign

for death? *Foreigner,*
I can't read his note

in full. Does he know
about the first boy

trained with mutes and levers,
then sent by foot to tune

against the island's brackish
air? Once, some learned

arpeggios; others,
fog and opium. A few climbed

cliffs and leapt, gave up
their bodies for water.

If there *is* a key
for this blue

island, it might be
B major—both gilt

and dark somehow,
what drifts now

from the open window:
someone loves Chopin's

third nocturne, even
in the height of day.

As I leave, I pass a school

where children clink
the first of their scales.

Zhǔ! From their teacher,
the only syllable

I can register. I think it is the *zhǔ*
that means *concentrate; join together.*

Or was it the other
one: *god; master?* Nuance:

all but the ferry's siren

dampens, meets the deaf
in my ear.

Length

Strange, all day I hadn't felt
or sung emptiness: 空

which is also how one writes
another word for empty:

air. Brisk, then
laden, it's spangled

with snowflakes, and I've forgotten,
until now, what snow

augments: absence. How
the gap between trees

A and B extends,
a scroll spread open,

how the theatrical pucker
of a Chinese roof won't

hush under white weight. How the character
for snow, 雪, is a full cloud

with a boar's-head
broom beneath it,

something we tried
to contain, to own

and, again, have
failed. Inside

in warmth, the woman
is pulling noodles, pale

threads of the cosmos—
this, our twisted lunch.

And everything I see
is larger than I thought.

And everything I've asked for
and more, I've been given.

At the Fortress

XINJIANG PROVINCE, THIRTEENTH CENTURY RUINS NEAR
THE CHINESE BORDERS WITH PAKISTAN, TAJIKISTAN,
AND AFGHANISTAN, 2010

The upslope flecked
with stray camels, earthen

domes—alone, I passed

Tajik tombs, emptied hives,
no sound.

Rock and sand
shifted hues: rust, amber, ash

to white. A snowstorm left behind
like unwound gauze,

or geist—and then the break

to alpine, where lakes
like organs gasped their blue.

Inside this lofted
wreck, what is said

to be a fortress,
I think, somehow,

in rooms; my steps mark

through dimensions. Here, I feel
the threshold, and then

a ward, facing west. A watch

towards what might
loom, whether horde or storm.

Already, could I know
this place—

if standing here,
would you? Why else, now,

would this arc
towards violence

cross me. Looking out
on what should be

blithe: sod, a lamb-dotted
moorland—I read fear

in Pamirs, the tops parched
and tied in cloud.

Who is to say
what remembrance

is, if just that
any fable, real

or imagined, would be
painted like this:

the stream, clear
as looking-glass, stones forced

into labyrinth,
a bridge over the moat?

I can say *watchtower*
and guess the first thing

that fell, but by
now, do we want to know

anything more
of fray. Whether I took

your arrow, or ate figs
out of your hand,

what is left? Teeth, and moldering

in the crenel—
is it more than wind

that instructs, tells me when
to cover my head.

Bleat: the warning now
across the open

grass—so wide,
I couldn't tell you

where the sound
began. But how

that vowel
comes at me—

undiluted, almost
human—I bend,

want to recant. But voice

draws me
in its augmenting

room. I thrum

against this charge:

here, coiled
in the throat,

air—the column—slits.

Notes and Glossary of Characters and Symbols

I.

"String Fugue with Stretto"

⌒ (fermata): in musical notation, a hold or pause; an indication of a note that is sustained longer than its value would suggest.

"Psalm: 1976" contains text from Psalm 119.

"To the Conservatory: 1983" contains text from Psalm 23, as well as a line from Olivia Newton John's 1981 hit, "Physical."

II.

"Elizabeth I, Richmond"

Italicized text is paraphrased from *The Language of Space in Court Performance, 1400–1625* by Janette Dillon, or else is quoted from Elizabeth I's poem "On Monsieur's Departure."

"A Road in the Sky"

This poem is inspired by May Swenson's poem, "Early Morning, Cape Cod."

III.

Many of these poems contain Chinese characters, or *hànzì*. The poems have simplified characters, which were introduced in mainland China in the 1950s and 1960s, and were the characters I was taught by my Mandarin teachers in Beijing and Shanxi.

Though some written characters still contain ideogrammic components, a limited number of Chinese characters exist as strict "pictograms," despite popular misconceptions. However, visual mimetics *are* sometimes used for teaching students to commit written characters to memory.

"A Map of Shanxi"
Shanxi Province is one of China's leading coal producers. The province contains several of the world's most polluted cities and also has severe water shortages.

gānzào: dry, arid.

"罗"
罗 *(luó):* a common Chinese surname. The traditional version is 羅, drawn as a net radical over two others, one meaning "bird" and one meaning "silk." In combination, they are meant to be read as "a net for catching birds."

易 *(yì):* "easy." Also a Chinese surname. In this poem, it is used strictly as onomatopoeia.

"In Mid-Autumn"
yuè bǐng: moon + a round, flat cake, cookie, or pastry; moon cake (food traditionally eaten on Mid-Autumn Day in China).

The syllable *bing* in Mandarin might mean "ice," "cake," "illness," or a number of other things, depending on whether it is pronounced with a high, rising, dipping, or falling tone.

"人 / 入 : A Redshift"
麻 *(má):* to have pins and needles, to feel numb.

"鼓浪屿"

鼓浪屿 *(gǔ làng yǔ):* "drum wave islet/island," a small island off the coast of Xiamen city.

Following China's loss in the First Opium War and the Treaty of Nanking in 1842, this island was settled by foreigners from eleven countries, and many churches and hospitals were established. Just under two square kilometers, the island contains over two hundred pianos, and is a popular tourist destination, as well as a source of national pride.

Konxinga (or Zheng Chenggong) was a military commander of the Ming dynasty. In mainland China, he is often considered a hero. He defeated the Dutch East India Company in Taiwan, thus re-establishing Chinese rule over the area.

喵喵 *(miāo miāo):* a peacock's shriek (onomatopoeic).